Con
ee

el autor

SEVEN WORDS OF HOPE

FRANK GONZÁLEZ

SEVEN WORDS OF HOPE

SPOKEN FROM THE CROSS

Pacific Press®
Publishing Association

Nampa, Idaho | Oshawa, Ontario, Canada
www.pacificpress.com

Cover design by Gerald Lee Monks
Cover design resources from Dreamstime.com
Inside design by Kristin Hansen-Mellish

Copyright © 2014 by Pacific Press® Publishing Association
Printed in the United States of America
All rights reserved

The author assumes full responsibility for the accuracy of all facts and quotations as cited in this book.

Unless otherwise noted, scriptures are quoted from the King James Version of the Bible.

Scriptures quoted from NEB are from *The New English Bible*, copyright © The Delegates of the Oxford University Press and the Syndics of the Cambridge University Press 1961, 1970. Reprinted by permission.

Texts credited to NIV are from the HOLY BIBLE, NEW INTERNATIONAL VERSION. Copyright © 1973, 1978, 1984 by International Bible Society, Inc. Used by permission of Zondervan Publishing House. All rights reserved.

Scriptures quoted from NKJV are from The New King James Version®, copyright © 1979, 1980, 1982 by Thomas Nelson, Inc. Used by permission. All rights reserved.

You can obtain additional copies of this book by calling toll-free 1-800-765-6955 or by visiting http://www.adventistbookcenter.com.

Library of Congress Cataloging-in-Publication Data:
González, Frank, 1957-
  Seven words of hope : spoken from the cross / Frank González.
     pages cm
  ISBN 13: 978-0-8163-5615-7 (hard cover)
  ISBN 10: 0-8163-5615-7 (hard cover)
 1. Jesus Christ—Crucifixion. 2. Jesus Christ—Seven last words. I. Title.
  BT457.G66 2014
  232.96'35—dc23
                                    2014037139

November 2014

Dedication

In memory of my mother,
Oneida María Batista y Brito de González,
by whose side I first learned to
"survey the wondrous cross
on which the Prince of glory died."

Contents

Introduction		9
Chapter 1	Forgiven	11
Chapter 2	Remembered	21
Chapter 3	Sheltered	35
Chapter 4	Delivered	47
Chapter 5	Refreshed	59
Chapter 6	Saved	67
Chapter 7	Triumphant!	77
Chapter 8	A Bonus Word: Grateful	85

Introduction

Have you ever wondered what the tallest pulpit in the world is—or in the entire universe for that matter? It is the cross of Jesus Christ!

He said that He would be "lifted up" so all the world—and the entire universe—could see Him and hear Him and thus be drawn to Him. No other voice has penetrated the ears of so many people as has the voice of Jesus, and nothing He said during the thirty-three-and-a-third years He spent among us is known as well as what He said while being crucified.

Jesus "preached" seven short sermons while on the cross. The mind-bending, heart-captivating, power-infusing, life-giving words of hope that He spoke there can give our souls the extreme makeover we have always wanted but thought we could not have. They can make us all truly whole and direct us to the best destiny we could ever have. I invite you to join me in exploring the riches of truth that these seven words of hope contain.

> Pastor Frank González
> Avon Park, Florida
> March 2014

Chapter 1

Forgiven

"Father, forgive them; for they know not what they do."
—Luke 23:34

I doubt that anyone other than Jesus ever preached from a pulpit like His. He preached a sermon—a one-sentence sermon—while He was being nailed to the cross. Actually, His "sermon" was a prayer. Jesus prayed for the soldiers who were driving nails through His wrist bones and His feet into the wooden beams of the cross. He said, "Father, forgive them; for they know not what they do" (Luke 23:34).

Was Jesus excusing those men for what they were doing? Was He saying that it didn't matter?

No, what they were doing was wrong, and He wasn't excusing it. He wasn't saying, "Go ahead; it's OK." In fact, His praying that they be forgiven was evidence that what they were doing was *terribly* wrong. It was a sin that called for repentance if they were to be saved.

The soldiers didn't know that what they were doing was sinful. *They didn't know who they were crucifying.* They thought Jesus looked innocent enough, but He must be a crazy fool, and the world would be better off without another crazy fool—so let's get on with the job.

They didn't know that they were murdering the Prince of life, the Savior of the world, the Messiah, the Lamb of God, the Son of God, the one who would be their Judge in the final trial. When Jesus prayed, "Father, forgive them," He was praying that the Holy Spirit would enlighten them and impress upon them how badly they needed a Savior.

The word *forgive* doesn't mean a mere pardon, or overlooking something with a wink, or whitewashing something that's wrong to make it seem right. No, in the original language, to *forgive* means to take a sin out of a person's heart.

In other words, Jesus was praying, "Father, don't hold this sin against these men because they don't realize who I am. But do convict them that it is a sin, so they will never want to do it again."

Jesus' prayer embraced Pontius Pilate, the Roman governor of Jerusalem and the surrounding area. Pilate had cowardly permitted Jesus to be killed because he was afraid the Jewish curia would accuse him to Caesar, and he might lose his job, which was a good one that paid him well.

Jesus' prayer encompassed also the Jewish high priest and the members of the ruling council of the Sanhedrin, who were ultimately responsible for Jesus' crucifixion. At Pentecost, the apostle Peter told them, "Ye denied the Holy One and the Just; . . . and killed the Prince of life" (Acts 3:14, 15). Those men hadn't nailed Jesus to the cross, yet they had more blood on their hands than all the soldiers put together. The hatred in their hearts was the problem. As the apostle Paul wrote, "The carnal mind is enmity against God; for it is not subject to the law of God, nor indeed can be" (Romans 8:7).

Though the men who crucified Jesus didn't realize it, they were acting out the essence of all the sins committed throughout all the ages. This evil world was using their hands to do the terrible deed, but deep down inside themselves, all humans are guilty of this sin.

The men who crucified Jesus were merely ordinary Roman soldiers who were paid to obey the orders of a centurion. Had you and I been where they were, it is likely that we would have done what they did. Not one of us is, by nature, any more righteous than were those pagans. As Martin Luther once put it, "We're all made of the same dough." And Paul said, "The whole world [is] accountable to God" (Romans 3:19, NIV).

We have no evidence that Jesus' prayer for Pilate actually was answered. He apparently died in misery, unrepentant. Nor have we any record that Caiaphas, the high priest, ever repented. While Jesus' prayer to His Father secured for them the gifts of repentance and salvation and all that goes with them, they could—and did—reject what He offered them. So they died as lost men—not because the Father wasn't willing to save them, but because they weren't willing to receive salvation from Him.

Their story was like Esau's. He *had* the birthright. It was his, and no one on earth or in heaven could take it from him. But he "despised" and "sold" what was given him. Thus he lost it forever. (See Genesis 25:34; Hebrews 12:16, 17.)

We can cherish the hope that some of the pagan Romans who didn't know what they were doing found repentance and salvation. No doubt we'll have some happy surprises after the first resurrection, for, as Matthew 27:54, tells us, "When the centurion and those with him, who were guarding Jesus, saw the earthquake and the things that had happened, they feared greatly, saying, 'Truly this was the Son of God!' " (NKJV).

In fact, we discover that that centurion, the officer in charge of the soldiers, did repent. Watching Jesus die did something to him. We read, "When the centurion saw what was done, he glorified God, saying, Certainly this was a righteous man" (Luke 23:47). When he heard Jesus give His first "word from the cross," that one-sentence "sermon" converted him!

God wants us to take courage. When we pray for someone, the Father hears our prayers. The centurion didn't confess his faith until after Jesus died; and it may take as long for our prayers for the conversion of someone we care about to be answered. But imagine how surprised and happy you will be on that day to see the fruit of "the travail of [your] soul" just as Jesus will at last see in the host of the redeemed the glorious answer to His prayer on the cross. Says Isaiah again, "He shall see of the travail of his soul, and shall be satisfied" (Isaiah 53:11).

Jesus' prayer on the cross was for you and me as well as for those pagan Roman soldiers. The entire human race is guilty of crucifying the Son of God. None of us has fully recognized who He is.

Isaiah described Jesus this way: "He hath no form nor comeliness; and when we shall see him, there is no beauty that we should desire him. [Note the prophet's constant use of the first-person pronouns *we* and *our*.] He is despised and rejected of men [that means *all* people]; a man of sorrows, and acquainted with grief: and we hid as it were our faces from him; he was despised, and we esteemed him not. . . . We did esteem him stricken, smitten of God, and afflicted" (Isaiah 53:2–4).

That "we" is you and I. Isaiah says that we, too, were totally mistaken about His identity.

It's true. Had we been there at that time and seen Him walk down the street carrying His carpentry tools, we wouldn't have given Him a second glance. But even during His incarnation, Jesus was still divine. He was the Son of God throughout His life on earth. Yet to save us, He laid aside the glory and privileges that were rightly His and became one of us.

When we're discussing this colossal case of mistaken identity, ignorance is no excuse. In stepping down from His high position in heaven to become one of us, Jesus identified Himself with every human being. So, when we trample over someone for any reason, we abuse Jesus Himself, for He says, "Inasmuch as ye have done it unto one of the least of these my brethren, ye have done it unto me" (Matthew 25:40).

The Bible clearly says that hatred is as bad as murder. Long before we pull the trigger on anyone, "He that loveth not his brother abideth in death. Whosoever hateth his brother *is a murderer*" (1 John 3:14, 15; emphasis added). If you hate, you're there already. When the right opportunity comes along, the public deed will reveal the hidden sin.

When we put all this together, we see a great truth: we have been guilty of crucifying Christ a thousand times! We desperately need to hear Him pray for us, "Father, forgive them: for they know not what they do."

A man and his wife stopped going to church after the pastor preached a sermon in which he spoke of "corporate guilt"—that is, that the sin of someone else could be put to our account but for the grace of Christ. He was making the point that everybody needs the Savior, and we do not know or realize the depth of sin that is lurking beneath the surface of our own hearts. We think we're OK, not knowing what we are capable of doing. "This offends us," the couple said. "We're not that bad."

Sometime later, the husband was out in the front

yard working on the lawn when a neighbor stopped by. The conversation turned sour, and the husband grabbed his shovel and was on the verge of lunging at his neighbor, when suddenly his face grew white, and he trembled, dropped the shovel, and fled into the house.

"Honey," he said, "I almost did it! I never dreamed I could become so angry!"

"Do you suppose that's what the pastor meant when he spoke of the evil that's buried in our hearts?" she asked.

When the next Sabbath came, they were in church again.

The prayer Jesus prayed from His cross unites us with the Father. When Jesus asked the Father to forgive us, He was also asking the Father to adopt us as His children; to make us His brothers and sisters.

James said, "The effectual fervent prayer of a righteous man availeth much" (James 5:16). How much more, then, a prayer of the Son of God Himself!

The Father heard the prayer Christ prayed in our behalf. We know this because Paul tells us, "The God and Father of our Lord Jesus Christ . . . hath made us accepted in the beloved" (Ephesians 1:3–6).

A woman had stopped attending church, but then

she heard that *La Voz de la Esperanza* (The Voice of Hope) was coming to her hometown to put on a program, and that proved to be something too difficult to pass by. She had been listening to the radio program as far back as she could remember.

She arrived a little late, and her heart sank when she saw that the place was full to the rafters. She was about to head back home when an usher approached her with good news. He knew where a seat was still available. He offered to usher her to that seat, and she agreed to follow him—something that she would soon regret.

Thankful that the usher had found her a seat, she sat down. But when she turned to greet the person next to her, a look of horror and disgust spread over her face. The woman she was sitting beside was the one who, years before, had stolen her husband! He had long since moved on to new conquests, but she held her seatmate more culpable than the rest because she had initiated him into his womanizing ways. Not wanting to draw attention to herself, however, she decided to stay and give her seatmate the coldest "cold shoulder" she could muster.

The sermon that day recounted the story of Mary Magdalene. It noted how Mary's encounter with Christ had given her the strength to forgive her abuser. The preacher went on to say that if victims harbor hatred and resentment, those feelings will bring injury and disease. By forgiving those who were torturing Him, Jesus kept His soul temple clean—and won the battle for our salvation.

At the end of the service, the woman whose husband had left her turned to her former enemy and said, "Go in peace, my sister. Christ has forgiven us both, and we should do the same!" Then the two women held each other in a long embrace as tears *and grace* flowed freely. The scene must have brought a smile to the face of Jesus Himself!

A wonderful song titled "Those Nails Were Mine" summarizes well what I have tried to say in this chapter. As its title suggests, this song says that each of us is responsible for Jesus' death. But He died so that we may have forgiveness.

Praise His name!

Chapter 2

Remembered

"And he said unto Jesus, Lord, remember me when thou comest into thy kingdom. And Jesus said unto him, Verily, I say unto thee today, thou shalt be with me in paradise."
—Luke 23:42, 43*

Some time ago I read a fascinating article about the *kodokushi* of Japan. *Kodokushi* is the name given to people who have lived and died alone, in perfect anonymity. Not having anyone to celebrate their presence or lament their absence and having left no record of themselves anywhere, they have come and gone without a trace. Vanished! Sayonara! It is estimated that there are more than a thousand kodokushi in Japan.

---

* The author has modified slightly the wording and punctuation of the King James Version of verse 43, placing the comma after the word *today* rather than after the word *thee*—for good reason, as will be demonstrated.

I suspect that Japan is not the only country with kodokushi. No doubt the list of the forsaken and forgotten is longer and comes closer to home than we care to admit. That some people should live such lives is as sad as it is unnecessary.

Does God treat some people as if they were kodokushi?

No doubt the men who were being crucified with Jesus thought He was like them. They even had biblical evidence for what they thought. After all, does not the Bible say that anyone dying on a cross is "accursed of God"? That means that such people are forsaken and forgotten forever by both God and man. (See Deuteronomy 21:22; Galatians 3:13.) In fact, the thieves heard the religious leaders of the Jews, the priests and rabbis, say things such as If you are the Son of God, come down from the cross! He saved others, but He cannot save Himself! "He trusted in God; let him deliver him now if he will have him; for he said, I am the Son of God." (See Matthew 27:40, 42–44.)

So for a while both thieves ridiculed Jesus. One kept at it to the bitter end; but the other began to watch and listen to Jesus. He heard the ridicule and saw that Jesus was able to take it all in stride with the nobility of a king. There was something inexpressibly noble about Him in this hour of His deep humiliation. Satan had hoped that Jesus' death on a cross would turn people against Him and against what He had taught them about God. How could anyone trust a Messiah who was so hopelessly condemned, so universally rejected?

Then, to his amazement, he heard Jesus say, "Father, forgive them: for they know not what they do." Jesus' plea that God would forgive the men who were torturing Him touched the heart of this thief. He thought, *This Man who is being crucified with us is really special. The kind of love He shows must come from God Himself. Could it be that the stories I've heard about Him are true? Could He be the Messiah for whom we've been waiting so long?*

But Jesus' words of love and forgiveness drew this thief past all of the roadblocks that Satan raised and brought him to faith. Though he was hanging on a cross, his heart was filled with deep joy as he concluded that the Man on the cross next to him was the Messiah. He actually was what the Samaritans called Him: "the Saviour of the world" (John 4:42). So the dying thief sent up a prayer that expressed his faith in Jesus. He prayed, "Lord, remember me when thou comest into thy kingdom" (Luke 23:42).

The answer that came from the lips of Jesus pleased the thief even more than hearing that he had won the lottery would have. Jesus promised, "Verily, I say unto thee today, thou shalt be with me in paradise" (verse 43).* The petition by the penitent thief and Jesus' response comprise the second of the seven words of hope that we're considering.

Oh, what a load rolled from this dying man's heart when Jesus spoke those words! It was as if Jesus had signed a check then and there that bought him a place in the first resurrection plus eternal life in Jesus' kingdom. That was worth more than all the gold in the entire world; more than all the pleasures it offered!

Knowing that his salvation was assured, the believing thief was no longer afraid to confess his sins and repent of them. Now he had the answers to the questions he had had about God. To his surprise he learned that God had always loved him. Now he can praise God for the great honor of being crucified with His Son. Now he knows that the Father regards him as though he had never sinned. And now he sees that all God's words and actions, all that He has done in his life, has come from His grace.

What is the thief's only regret? That he hadn't known the good news of God's grace till now. The words of Jesus have lifted from his soul the awful

---

* Again, the wording and punctuation have been changed. I'll explain shortly.

feeling of being cursed by God. There's no better place in the whole world for a person to be than with Jesus, the Son of God—even if that means being crucified with Him (see Galatians 2:20).

Please note what Jesus did *not* say or do. He didn't say, "If you'll be good and do everything just right from now on, then I will save you in My kingdom!" No, Jesus never bargains with us. He says only that we must believe Him, have faith in Him, trust Him. He treated this thief in just the same way as He had treated Abraham. Genesis 15:5, 6 says Abraham "believed in the LORD; and he counted it to him for righteousness." When he chose to believe, his heart changed.

Jesus made the same "new covenant" with the dying thief. He didn't require anything of the thief. When the thief saw Jesus' love and His forgiving spirit, his heart was won and he believed—and the Lord counted that as righteousness. Note that when Jesus made this all-important promise, the thief was saved at that very moment, that very day. There was nothing else he needed to do. No ritual he needed to perform. He had Jesus' promise right then.

But that didn't mean he was headed to Paradise that day.

A someday promise made "today"

We need to take a careful look at this part of the story. The New King James Version says Jesus told the dying thief, "Assuredly, I say to you, today you will be with Me in Paradise [heaven]" (Luke 23:43, NKJV), and most other versions say the same thing, though the wording varies a little. They all picture Jesus promising the thief that they would both be in heaven that very day.

But Jesus didn't go to heaven that day. In fact, even after His resurrection on Sunday morning, He told Mary not to cling to Him because, He said, "I have not yet ascended to My Father" (John 20:17, NKJV). So, the dying thief couldn't have gone to heaven with Jesus on the Friday when they were crucified because on the following Sunday morning Jesus said He hadn't been there yet.

Does this mean that the Bible contradicts itself? Do we have to choose one Gospel and reject the other?

No. There's a simple answer to this apparent contradiction. The men who wrote the four Gospels—Matthew, Mark, Luke, and John—wrote them in Greek long before punctuation was invented. So the part of the verse with which we're concerned looked like this (except it was in Greek rather than English): "I say unto thee today thou shalt be with me . . ." When there's no comma present, we can put the emphasis wherever we believe it should go. If we put the comma after the word *thee,* then the verse says Jesus promised the thief that the two of them would be in heaven that very day—and the Gospels of Luke and John contradict each other.

But if we put the comma after the word *today* instead of after the word *thee,* the passage says that Jesus was making a promise that very day—the day of their crucifixion, when the future looked pretty dark. He was promising that despite what seemed to be a total and final defeat for Him and for those who had cast their lot with Him, the day was coming when all of them—including the repentant thief—would be in heaven with Jesus.

In other words, Jesus was saying,

> *"Today, when I seem to be an utter failure,*
> *today,* when the world despises Me,
> *today,* when even my Father appears to have forsaken Me,
> *today,* when we're nailed to wooden beams

and cannot confirm our covenant with
a handshake,
today, I assure you of eternal salvation with
Me 'in Paradise.' "

The Bible says that death is like a sleep. When Jesus' friend Lazarus died, Jesus told His disciples, "Our friend Lazarus sleepeth, but I go, that I may awake him out of sleep." The disciples assumed that Lazarus's fever had diminished and he was taking a nap, so they thought that he was improving. Then Jesus said plainly, "Lazarus is dead" (John 11:11–14).

Paul tells us that all of the believers who have died before Jesus returns "sleep" until His coming, when He will resurrect them never to die again. And Paul adds that this blessed truth is a "comfort" to know and to believe (1 Thessalonians 4:14–18).

The prophet Daniel also connects the "death as a sleep" idea with this great resurrection: "Many of them that sleep in the dust of the earth shall awake. . . . And they that be wise shall shine as the brightness of the firmament" (Daniel 12:2, 3).

So, according to the Bible, no one is suffering now in either hell or purgatory; and, except for some special cases, no one has gone to heaven yet either—which is a mercy, for if our family and friends went to heaven when they died, just imagine how painful it would be for them to see the suffering of their loved ones who were still living on the earth.

No, the dead are asleep. They rest, quietly unconscious, until the Savior awakens them. He said, "The hour is coming in which all who are in the graves will hear His voice and come forth—those who have done good, to the resurrection of life, and those who have done evil, to the resurrection of condemnation" (John 5:28, 29).

On this precious "today" that God has given us, we can choose which of these two resurrections we'll experience. The same Savior who loved the repentant thief loves you and me too. He assures us that He died that awful death on the cross so that we, unworthy though we are, never have to suffer the "second death" (see John 5:24).

If, like the believing thief, you look back on your life with spiritual insight, you'll see that ever since you were a baby, God has loved you. The truth is that He gave His only begotten Son for you so that you need never "perish." Thank Him for that love; believe the promise that He makes to you today that you will be with Him in Paradise!

How I learned that God loves me

Forrest Gump's mom warned Forrest that life is like a box of chocolates "because you never know what you're gonna get." You don't have to be physically and/or mentally challenged to relate to that. We all have some chocolates in our boxes that are filled with yucky stuff.

If, like me, you were a teenager with a Spanish surname growing up in the South during the 1960s, you pretty much knew that you were going to get some of those chocolates that are filled with yucky stuff.

On an otherwise uneventful sunny Sunday afternoon in a middle-class neighborhood in Orlando, Florida, I came close to having to sample some chocolates that were filled with pretty bad stuff. For no reason other than my family's unfortunate move into a neighborhood that was all Anglo, I found myself surrounded by a bunch of angry young men carrying sticks and chains in their hands and hatred in their hearts. They formed a circle around me—but they weren't planning for us to hold hands and sing, "We Shall Overcome."

Clearly, they were angry, but so was I—though not at them. All my anger was directed at the big White-Bearded Guy in the sky.

The neighbors came out to see what all the fuss was about. *Good!* I thought. *Someone will call the police.* But then I realized that our neighbors were applauding the mob, and I knew that meant that I was in trouble.

My cousin, two years my junior, took off running. Don't judge him too harshly. He was no coward. He went to get Rambo.

Don't laugh. I'm not talking about the movie guy. I mean a *real-life* Rambo! Our oldest cousin—who lived around the corner and two blocks down the street—was a Green Beret soldier who had just finished a tour of duty in Vietnam. He had what they called "Vietnam syndrome," which meant that occasionally he thought he was back in the war. His home was a virtual military arsenal. He had an M16 rifle, and—get this—even live grenades! He wasn't home, though, so I was on my own.

Never was a sunny day so gloomy. I wished I was Speedy González, not Frank González. Then I could have left my assailants behind in a cloud of dust. But I wasn't, so only one Person could save me now. Yes, God. He was my only hope. But there was one big problem: He and I were not on speaking terms.

Before I tell you what ensued, a little background is in order. You need to know how an altar boy had come to hate God the way I did. It was rather simple. My father was a political prisoner, and ever since I was four years old, I had prayed every night for him to be released. Somehow, God had managed to ignore my prayers for thirteen years. It was because of that lack of action that I had given up on prayer and on God.

My mother had come to God's defense. She said getting God to answer your prayer was like going to the barbershop: you take a number and wait your turn. My prayers hadn't been answered yet because God was swamped with petitions and my number hadn't come up yet.

I wondered where I stood in heaven's line now!

Then I remembered what Mr. Paulín had said a couple days ago as he was studying the Bible with an uncle of mine who was a pediatrician. Mr. Paulín said angels are servants of God whom He sends to care for His people. He even said that it is likely that each of us has a guardian angel whose full-time job is to protect us.

I wondered whether any of that was true. It suddenly had become a matter of life or death.

So I swallowed my pride and turned to God. But I wasn't about to be a hypocrite. I was still angry at God, and I wasn't about to pretend otherwise. I said,

"Look, God, I don't know where my number is on the line, but if You have any interest whatsoever in Frank González, I suggest this is as good a time as any to show it. And that angel I'm supposed to have? He'd better show up pronto!"

At that time, my would-be assailants launched themselves at me—only to be repelled by some unseen force that left them unhurt except for their pride. Before long they got in their cars and on their motorcycles and disappeared, and they never bothered me again.

This experience began a new life for me—a life in which I was keenly aware of God's presence, His love, and His plan for me. Later, I learned that in order to be able to intervene in my life, God had to allow His Son to be attacked by evil forces without any friendly, angelic intervention. Jesus endured that alone, taking upon Himself the condemnation that we deserved so He could become our Savior.

My friend, Jesus loves everyone. He loves *you*. He wants to promise you that, like the thief on the cross, you'll be with Him in Paradise. If you ask Him to, He'll make something incredible out of your box of chocolates. Are you ready to open the box and begin to taste the good things that it contains?

Chapter 3

Sheltered

*"Jesus . . . saith unto his mother, Woman, behold thy son!
Then saith he to the disciple, Behold thy mother!"
—John 19:26, 27*

No other woman is so highly honored as is the virgin Mary. For nine months she carried in her womb the One whose name is "Emmanuel, which being interpreted is, God with us" (Matthew 1:23). This means that not only was her Son, Jesus, truly a human being (for He became one of us), but He was also the divine Son of God. He is the bridge that joins lost humanity to God. Being one of us, He knows all about us. The Bible says that in His humanity He was "in all points tempted like as we are, yet without sin" (Hebrews 4:15).

Jesus came from heaven with a sinless nature. Yet He took upon Himself our sinful human nature so that He could understand our temptations. Thus, He is "touched with the feelings of our infirmities" (Hebrews 4:15), for He knows how weak we are.

Jesus was "made like unto his brethren" (Hebrews 2:17). We have sinful natures, but through the miracle of the new birth, the Holy Spirit can cover them with Christ's sinless nature.

How close is Jesus to us? Did He know family love as we know it? Did He humble Himself to obey the commandments despite having been their Author? How did He relate to His earthly mother?

Although He was God in human flesh, the divine Commander of the heavenly angels, He humbled Himself as a child to be "subject" unto His mother Mary, even though she could not understand Him and sometimes made life difficult for Him. On one occasion she scolded Him for something that was her fault, not His.

Jesus and His parents had traveled to Jerusalem to attend the Passover. When the services were over and they headed home, Mary carelessly assumed that Jesus was somewhere in the group with whom they were traveling. But when nightfall came and she began to look for Him, she couldn't find Him.

Remembering that King Herod had once tried to

kill Him, she panicked and rushed back to Jerusalem with Joseph, looking for Jesus. She finally found Him in the temple theological seminary, reasoning with the great teachers of Israel (at the age of twelve!). "And all who heard Him were astonished at His understanding and answers" (Luke 2:47, NKJV).

When the people who found Jesus brought Him to her, she voiced her annoyance. "Son," she said, "why hast thou thus dealt us? behold, thy father and I have sought thee sorrowing" (verse 48). In other words, why have You been so naughty?

Jesus hadn't been naughty, but He responded courteously to her ill temper. "How is it that ye sought me? wist ye not that I must be about my Father's business? And they understood not the saying which he spake unto them" (verses 49, 50).

What this twelve-year-old said went right over their heads. In Jesus' case, that wasn't unusual. It was a regular happening. Even His mother frequently misunderstood Him. (By the way, did you notice that at twelve years old, Jesus already knew that God Himself was His Father?)

We would be tempted to act a little resentfully toward a parent who misunderstood us often, but Jesus' love for His mother never wavered. He obeyed the fifth of the Ten Commandments: "Honor thy father and thy mother" (Exodus 20:12). It doesn't tell us to ignore them if we think they don't deserve our honor.

Jesus forgave Mary for all her fretting and scolding even though it sometimes made life difficult for Him—just as scolding, fretful parents can make life difficult for us. (And yes, Jesus forgives the overworked mothers and fathers of today who scold their children too frequently.)

Arrested, condemned, and crucified

Eventually, Jesus was arrested by the temple police and then condemned and nailed to a cross to die. The pain of the nails in His wrists and ankles was unspeakably hard to bear in itself; but add to the physical pain the shame He had to endure and the weight of the sins of the world that rolled upon His heart.

Jesus heard the jeering of the priests and the mob, and it, too, brought Him pain. But though it was excruciating, He remembered also that God is love and that He was the Son of God. So, even though He was suffering on the cross, the love in His heart must find expression. That's what moved Him to pray for His enemies and then to minister to the penitent thief who was being crucified with Him.

Now we hear His third "word" from the cross. Though wracked with pain, He remembers His brokenhearted mother, who is standing by the cross with the disciple John. They are bewildered by what is happening; they can't begin to fathom it all. Why did Jesus let them crucify Him when He knows He is the Messiah?

Mary is devastated. Can this man who is dying like a criminal be her Son—the One she carried in her womb? Didn't the angel Gabriel tell her that God was His Father?

She remembered that John the Baptist called Him "the Lamb of God," that the Samaritans said He was "the Savior of the world," and that before Jesus' birth the angel Gabriel assured Mary, "He shall save his people from their sins" (Matthew 1:21).

He is the only hope for the salvation of the world. Must God's great plan of salvation be ruined by this unspeakable tragedy? No other mother has ever known the same pain!

But Jesus has not lost His regal bearing. He speaks as we would expect the Commander of the angel hosts to speak. Looking at His mother with tender pity, He nods His head toward John and says, "Woman, behold thy son. Then saith he to the disciple, Behold thy mother" (John 19:26, 27). The love Jesus felt for His mother brought to His lips this third "word of hope"—this third "sermon" that Jesus "preached" from His cross.

Here we see Jesus obeying the fifth commandment even as He is dying in agony. We see Him honoring His mother before the world. We see Him forgiving her for her faults and failings. We see Him thanking her for her loving care.

In honoring Mary, Jesus honored every mother in the world. In effect, He said, "I appreciate your motherhood; your devotion to your children; the sacrifices you made for their betterment; your never ending love for them."

Jesus loves every mother in the world. Mothers who have too much work to do, or unruly children, or worries about providing for their children, or other heartaches and problems need to remember how the dying Son of God provided for His mother and to realize that He cares just as much for her too. Yes, mothers, you are sheltered by His love.

Every child is unruly and disobedient at times. And there is probably not a mother in the world who, when her children act that way, hasn't been tempted to become cross. When a person works, works, works—doing the laundry, the housekeeping, the dishes, and more—and, as is often the case today, also has a job outside her home, oh, how heavy the burdens become! Then a mother's nerves become taut, and her spirit chafes, and she wonders how it can be said that God loves her when He has permitted all this to overwhelm her.

And when—as is all too often the case—she is a single mom, these burdens and questions are multiplied.

No doubt Mary wondered what would happen to her now. Was Jesus leaving her alone in the world?

But even as Jesus hung on cross, He gave Mary good news. He put her in the care of John, "the disciple whom He loved." In doing so, He did more to provide for Mary's future than He would have if He had given her a bank account that contained more than a million dollars.

The Savior's greatest delight today is telling mothers that He will provide for their future. You will find great peace if you will believe that He cares for you.

How great was the blessing that John and his family received by taking care of Jesus' mother for the rest of her life! She probably shared stories about the boyhood of Jesus. This may have helped John when he wrote his wonderful gospel and the three letters to the church he pastored.

The prodigal daughter

A clock radio switched on at just the right time to stop a mother when she was about to pull the trigger of a gun she was aiming at her only daughter. And she was a good mother!

Back to the beginning.

This woman had a gun and knew how to use it because she was a soldier in the Nicaraguan army. She had joined the armed forces for a good reason: so she could become tough enough to protect herself and her daughter. She felt this to be a necessity when her husband ran off and left her to raise their daughter by herself.

It turned out that the military lifestyle suited her temperament and personality. She climbed quickly through the ranks, so she was able to provide for her daughter's upbringing and pay for private schooling.

Life was good. But the fairy tale was about to go terribly wrong—becoming more like a horror story from Hollywood hell.

As this woman's daughter entered her late teens,

she developed a taste for partying with her friends late into the night. And nothing her mother said or did to correct her worked. Of course, alcohol was a part of that lifestyle, and it, in turn, led to drugs, which, horror of horrors, led to prostitution so that she could feed the heroin addiction that had run amok.

The girl's mother was devastated. She had worked so hard for so long—only to find that it had been for naught. She had endured the long hours of study and the rigors of a military life because she wanted to provide a good future for her little girl, who was her one reason to live. And now her daughter was a—what?

The woman thought about killing herself. However, the hope, albeit remote, of her daughter coming to her senses and returning home kept her going.

Her daughter did come home, but the actuality could not have been further from what she had hoped for. When her daughter appeared at her door, she was a mere shadow of her former self. She was dying. She had full-blown AIDS, and she was little more than a sack of nerves and bones with the life zapped out of them.

But the woman had prayed long for this moment, and now that it had come, she tried to make the most of it. She took her daughter into her arms, and her tears flowed like Niagara Falls.

Days, weeks, and months passed, and the daughter suffered the horrors of the slow, fatal disease that AIDS was at that time. Night after endless night, blood-curdling screams came from her daughter's room, interspersed with cries for help: "Mom, the pain, the pain! *Do* something. Please *do* something!"

Then came the night when the mother had believed she had suffered enough, and she felt that her daughter had suffered enough too. That is when she armed herself with a gun and built up the courage to do the unthinkable. She intended to put an end to her daughter's misery and then to her own—which brings us full circle to the beginning of our story. It was precisely at the moment that the mother had gained the courage she needed to commit the macabre act that the clock radio switched on.

God used that clock radio to subject this military mother to a friendly invasion. From its speaker came *La Voz de la Esperanza* (The Voice of Hope). The message that program carried through the air brought this desperate mother and her dying daughter to the cross of Christ, to Bible studies, and eventually to baptism, through which they both confessed publicly their faith in Jesus Christ, the Savior of the world.

Later, a letter found its way to our offices in Simi

Valley, California. In it the mother happily shared with us this remarkable story of how the love of God reached down and found her in the moment of her greatest need. She told us that her daughter had passed away, but that for many months before her death she had a reprieve from the pain she had been suffering, giving the two of them the opportunity to spend many happy and precious moments together. Even better, though, was the assurance that they both could look forward to Christ's second coming and life everlasting.

Yes, Jesus is the Savior of the world—in Nicaragua and all around the globe. He can be *your* Savior, too, no matter *where* you are!

Chapter 4

Delivered

"My God, my God, why hast thou forsaken me?"
—Matthew 27:46

How close has God Himself come to us here in our earthly darkness?

Loneliness—the feeling of being alone or of having nothing in common with the people around you—is one of the most painful of human feelings. A bright spring morning in a place filled with flowers can seem dark when there's no one near us with whom we can share the beauty. That's why we can feel lonely even when we're in the middle of a large crowd in a big city.

Imagine that you're guilty of having committed some serious sin and have been condemned to live alone in total darkness forever. Your guilt shuts you away from God's approval; you see only His anger and abhorrence. And not only does God condemn you, but you also condemn yourself. What word describes such a horrible situation?

Only one word: *hell*.

Fortunately, God has made it possible for us to avoid experiencing that kind of hell. However, occasionally imagining how that makes us feel may serve a good purpose in that it could help us to appreciate the deliverance God has provided us through the cross of our Lord Jesus Christ.

For people who lived in the days of ancient Israel, death on the cross was inextricably bound up with hell. God told Moses that criminals who were found to be guilty of a capital crime and who were executed by death on a "tree" were to be considered "accursed of God."*

Everybody believed that to be true. That's why when Joab, one of King David's generals, found the rebel prince Absalom hanging in a tree, he considered this to be evidence that God had cursed Absalom, so he felt free to shoot Absalom full of arrows despite the king's request. (See 2 Samuel 18.)

The teaching of Moses that death by hanging meant

---

* Interestingly, the ancient Hebrew says "he who is hanged *is* the curse of God"; see Deuteronomy 21:22, 23.

the criminal bore the curse of God also explains why the Jewish rulers begged Pilate to have Jesus crucified rather than to have Him stoned. They believed that if they could get Jesus executed by hanging, His fellow citizens would forever have considered Him to have been convicted of crimes beyond imagination. That would have suggested to them that God had cursed Him, and that would have ended His mission forever.

The crowds of people who came to Jesus' cross to laugh at Him and to jeer and taunt Him were motivated by this general belief that anyone hung to die on a cross was a human write off—a piece of junk like an old car that's been discarded and now can do nothing more than to be the target of stone-throwing kids. They felt free to treat Him as they wished—to spit on Him, to throw rotten eggs and tomatoes at Him, to revile Him, to curse Him. It seemed like they felt they could prove their loyalty to God by their inhumanity to this man who was abandoned even by His disciples, His friends!

Let's not fool ourselves by picking up a wrong idea here. We have no right to assume that Jesus was too wise to be hurt by this condemnation. Though He never sinned, He humbled Himself so He could become one of us (see Philippians 2). When Jesus was on the cross, "the LORD . . . laid on him the iniquity of us all" (Isaiah 53:6). There God "made him . . . , who knew no sin," to be sin for us (2 Corinthians 5:21), and He drank the whole cup of the wrath of God—something that no other human had ever tasted (see Matthew 20:22; John 18:11). This means that Jesus felt all that being crucified entailed. Isaiah wrote that the anguish He suffered was so strong that it even changed His physical appearance! His face became so terribly distorted that we wouldn't have recognized Him as being human (see Isaiah 52:14).

In the midnightlike blackness that enveloped the cross, Jesus couldn't help but cry out in the most awful of bloodcurdling screams, "My God, my God, why hast thou forsaken me?" (Matthew 27:46). These words comprise the fourth minisermon that Jesus preached from His cross.

How could the sinless Son of God ever utter such a cry of despair?

He could because the guilt of every human being who has ever lived was crushing His human heart as though tons of stone were piled upon it. No one else had ever felt such a burden, nor has anyone felt it since. No one—not even the vilest of criminals—has yet died the second death. That comes only at the end of the thousand years of Revelation 20; the end of the final judgment.

In fact, we can honestly say that Jesus Christ is the only human ever to have *really* experienced death. All the billions of others who have "died" have simply gone to sleep.

The fact is that the Bible speaks of two kinds of death, and the death that Jesus died is the real thing. It's the one with eternal consequences. It's the "second death" that is mentioned in Revelation 2:11 and 20:14. Yet, no human other than the Savior, Jesus, the Lamb of God, has died the second death (see Hebrews 2:9). He is the only actual "Lamb of God." All the other lambs that have been sacrificed for human sins were only types or symbols of the real Lamb of God. And even rivers of animal blood could never purchase forgiveness for one human sin. Only the death of the Son of God could provide such forgiveness.

In the Garden of Eden, God told Adam and Eve that sin would mean death because sin is lethal in and of itself. Just as the roots of a full-grown tree reach deep down into the earth, sin reaches deep within us, permeating our very being. We can find deliverance from sin only by seeing what the Son of God had to suffer in order to pay its penalty, and only by trusting that it is sufficient.

Jesus' sacrifice paid the penalty of the broken law. However—and this has been the scandal of apostate Christianity for nearly two thousand years—merely being forgiven would leave us as selfish and sinful as we were before we turned to Him were not our sinful hearts changed.

Real faith

How can our sinful hearts be changed?

The Bible says, "As Moses lifted up the serpent in the wilderness, even so must the Son of man be lifted up: that whosoever believeth in him should not perish, but have eternal life" (John 3:14, 15).

Moses lifted up an image of a snake, and those who looked upon it in faith were healed—for the time being. But the look that means life—eternal life—for us is the look that is directed in faith at the Man who was elevated on a cross so that we could see Him and be healed. The crucifixion of Christ is more than a legal maneuver through which He paid the penalty laid on us when we sinned. When we see Christ raised on the cross, we "comprehend with all saints what is the breadth, and length, and depth, and height" of His love, "which passeth knowledge," and we actually become "filled with all the fulness of God" (Ephesians 3:18, 19).

It is the "comprehending" that does it. As one very wise man put it, "When I survey the wondrous cross on which the Prince of glory died, my richest gain I count but loss, and pour contempt on all my pride."

We "survey" the cross by looking at it frequently with our eyes and our hearts wide open. Then, like little children trying to grasp something far bigger than they can imagine, we begin to comprehend what has happened—that the divine Son of God, our Creator, has become our Savior. In a sense, He has become you and He has become me. When He died on that cross, I died with Him, for He has taken my humanity and borne my sin. And since He has identified with me, I begin to identify with Him. So, like Paul, I can say, "I am crucified with Christ" (Galatians 2:20).

All right-minded people say "Thank you" when someone does them a favor. How much more, then, should those who accept what Christ did on that cross say a huge "Thank You!" to God for this sacrifice. That is what Jesus meant when He said that whoever believes in Him will not perish—will not die the second death—but will instead have eternal life. Faith includes a deep appreciation for the love that moved the Son of God to go to hell for us—to die the second death for us!

Faith isn't merely the purchasing of an insurance policy that guarantees your safety when fire covers the earth but that leaves your heart as cold as stone. Genuine faith is something expressed by the heart; it must mean a change of heart. It is something that "worketh by love" (Galatians 5:6).

Such faith can never stand alone. It has to do something immediately. It produces obedience to all the commandments of God, including the seventh commandment and the fourth commandment (which is overlooked week after week by the majority of professed Christians).

Those who believe never forget what hell is. They never forget that awful, eternal loneliness—and that Jesus saved them from it. In return, they say "Thanks!" and they consecrate their lives, their all, to the One who died for them, to the One who went through hell for them.

The Holy Spirit inspired a song to enable us to understand the pain Jesus felt when it seemed that both His heavenly Father and His earthly friends forsook Him. We know this song as Psalm 22. It reveals to us the mind of the crucified Savior and shows the psychological progression He made—how He survived His trial by fire. And while Jesus' experience is unique and unrepeatable, it does reveal what we can do when we face our final trial. We might call this song, which has three stanzas, "Out of the Darkness and Into the Light."

Stanza 1

The first verse of this psalm reveals that Jesus was honest and open with God. He told His Father how He really felt. This psalm begins with a cry of despair, "My God, my God, why hast thou forsaken me?" Those words expressed the despair Jesus felt at the apparent desertion of His heavenly Father as well as of His disciples.

We, too, must be honest and open with God. He wants only the truth from us: our true selves, our genuine sentiments.

We might feel that like Jesus, we, too, have been forsaken; but in our case it is usually because our spiritual eyesight is failing us. Jesus has promised that He will never leave us nor forsake us (see Hebrews 13:5).

In verse 2 Jesus says He called for His Father day and night, but it seemed that His Father didn't hear or didn't care to answer. Verse 6 tells us how this apparent rejection made Jesus feel. He cried, "I am a worm, and no man; a reproach of men, and despised of the people."

Jesus knows from experience how the down-and-out feel.

Verses 7 and 8 picture people laughing at Jesus—mocking Him and saying, "He trusted on the Lord that He would deliver Him. If He is the Son of God, let God deliver Him!" This was the cruelest cruelty. Jesus could have saved Himself, but if He had, He couldn't have saved humanity.

Stanza 2

Verses 9 and 10 reveal Jesus reviewing His life, starting with His birth in Bethlehem. When He was only a baby, God delivered Him. Jesus would have died right at the beginning if His Father hadn't saved Him.

When you are discouraged, remember the times when the Lord has delivered you. This is spiritual warfare in which you must persevere—and you can if you depend on Jesus for strength.

In Jesus' prayer as recorded in verse 11, He says, "There is none to help." He is dreadfully alone! And verse 14 provides the diagnosis: Jesus is suffering what we would call a nervous breakdown. But He can't give in to it! He can't close His eyes in sleep! He must endure the horrors of the second death.

Verses 16 and 18 portray the progression toward His death. "They pierced My hands and My feet. . . . They divide My garments among them, and for My clothing they cast lots" (NKJV). (Just so we are clear, remember that this is about Jesus on the cross. It isn't simply David speaking.)

So, what does Jesus do?

Stanza 3

The old gospel song says, "Turn your eyes upon Jesus." That is what *we* need to do. But *Jesus* needed to turn His eyes to the pain and poverty of others: to those who were torturing Him, to the penitent thief, to His mother, and to you and me!

Verse 20 tells us that Jesus calls upon God to "deliver [His] soul from the sword; [His] darling from the powers of the dog."* Who is Jesus' "precious"? Who is His "darling"? Those for whom and to whom He gave His life: you and me! It is us! It was the thought of His rescue of you and me and the redeemed of all

---
* Where the King James Version has *darling,* the New King James Version has *precious.*

the ages that gave Jesus the strength to carry on. The rest of Psalm 22 is a song of victory.

While we don't suffer the agony that Jesus felt, we do suffer pain. In order to succeed, we need to turn our attention to the pain and the need of our fellow human beings, our brothers and sisters in Christ, because Christ has delivered all of us from the hellish horrors of the second death.

Our hearts are so small; we are so narrow in our thinking and feeling. But just saying Thank You in appreciation for His sacrifice on His cross stretches us a bit. And wonder of wonders, we then begin learning how to love as He loves. And then His love comes full circle!

Yes, Jesus Christ has made it possible for us to sing in our darkest nights the song of faith He authored and finished during those agonizing hours on the cross. So sing, my friend! Sing!

Chapter 5

Refreshed

"I thirst."—John 19:28

If your worst enemy were thirsty, would you give him a drink? I hope so. Giving someone a drink is the most elemental of all human courtesies. That is because thirst is far more difficult for any human or animal to bear than is hunger. Wild animals in Africa will do anything in time of drought to get at some wet mud so they can extract a little moisture. All creatures on earth must have water.

Has God ever known what it is to be thirsty? Well, we know that the Son of God did experience thirst. One hot day as He was traveling some eighty miles on foot, He passed through Sychar, a Samaritan village. It was lunchtime, so the disciples went to the market to buy some groceries, and while they did so, Jesus rested near a well.

Jesus was thirsty, and He was near a well, but He

had nothing with which to draw water from the well. He could have spoken a word and an angel would have brought him a drink, but He didn't do that. The rules that governed His life on earth forbade Him from doing anything that we can't do.

So the Creator of the world and all the water on it sat there helpless, hoping someone would come to get some water and would offer Him a drink. Yes, the Son of God knew thirst as well as we do!

Incidentally, John says that a Samaritan woman did come to draw water, and Jesus did ask her for a drink. But then their conversation so captured her attention that she left without giving Him any water. So, apparently, when this encounter ended, Jesus was still thirsty. But that's not my point here.

Scripture tells us about one other time when Jesus was thirsty. That was when He was nailed on a cross and about to die.

When Jesus was crucified, He suffered the most excruciating pain—both mental and physical—that any human has ever endured. Crucifixion was the most diabolical method of executing criminals that any government has ever invented. It was intended to prolong the agonized suffering of the victim as long as possible and to expose the poor wretch who was being crucified to public humiliation. Jesus had to endure all this in order to save us.

When the soldiers nailed His wrist bones and ankles to the wooden beams of the cross, some people with a bit of pity in their souls offered Him a drink of wine into which a painkiller drug had been mixed. A Roman historian tells us that this was the custom when criminals were executed. Apparently, some ladies' aid groups felt moved by human pity to do this. But when they offered this primitive analgesic to Jesus, He refused to drink it.

That drug-bearing wine was an enormous temptation to Jesus. He knew the pain He was facing would be intense. (It already was!) It would have been so refreshing just to gulp down the wine and the painkiller and go to sleep. Being up all night and enduring beatings and a scourging that lacerated His back and caused a serious loss of blood made the relief that the concoction offered tempting.

But the world's most crucial hour had come. Though Jesus was nailed to a cross, He had a task to accomplish. He was working for the salvation of all the people who had ever lived and who would ever live. He was to be the sacrifice that would provide forgiveness to all who would ask for it. But to do so, He must be without sin.

That meant He needed to keep His mind clear and all His senses alert so that He would make no mistake of any kind—even as seemingly inconsequential as speaking a wrong word or thinking a wrong thought. The salvation of untold millions of people was in the balance during that fearful hour. That is why Jesus resisted this temptation. That's why He said No to the offer of pain-killing wine.

Let's pause here for just a moment to note an important reason why we, too, must be temperate in all things. Alcohol and drugs becloud our minds, and eating too much can do the same. Our Savior refused a drink that would have hindered Him as He fought the battle to save us. We, too, must keep our minds clear. We need to be able to understand and appreciate what He accomplished. So Jesus pleads with us just now, "Keep a watch on yourselves; do not let your minds be dulled by dissipation and drunkenness . . . so that the great Day closes upon you suddenly like a trap" (Luke 21:34, NEB).

When Jesus was dying

Later, as death drew near, Jesus again spoke of being thirsty. By this time He had endured the terrible sense of loneliness that He felt when it seemed to Him that His Father had forsaken Him. He had borne the almost impossible burden of the sins of the whole world. He had kept His mind clear, refusing every temptation Satan had brought. By faith He had broken through the darkness and had won the great victory. But the conflict had exhausted Him, and now His body cried out again for relief, so He said, "I thirst" (John 19:28). How He would have loved a drink of cool, fresh water from a spring—like the water we take for granted; the water that comes to us as a precious gift from God!

Right here we find a tiny bit of good news about somebody who chose to respond in kindness to Jesus' need. Unfortunately, this kind gesture didn't come from the men who claimed to be the spiritual leaders of God's people of that day. Their hatred knew no end. Nor do we read that even one of the eleven disciples who remained ran to get water to relieve Jesus' thirst. Instead, Scripture tells us that one or more of the pagan soldiers took pity on Him as a fellow human being who was suffering. John's Gospel says, "There was set a vessel full of vinegar: and they filled a sponge with vinegar, and put it upon hyssop, and put it to his mouth" (verse 29).

Those soldiers offered Him a drink that was free of

painkilling drugs. Note that John wrote that "all things" Scripture specified about Jesus' sacrifice had now been fulfilled (verse 28). His work was done; now He could rest. So we read that Jesus "received the vinegar."

Earlier in His ministry, Jesus had said, "Whosoever shall give you a cup of water to drink in my name, because ye belong to Christ, verily I say unto you, he shall not lose his reward" (Mark 9:41). We don't know the name of the Roman soldier who brought Jesus a drink when He was thirsty; but he fits into the category of people who receive a blessing for their every act of kindness to someone who suffers.

The soldier couldn't earn his salvation by giving a drink to Jesus; but his kind act proved that his heart had something in it that was warm and tender in spite of the horrible job he had. What he saw at Jesus' crucifixion may have already begun to grow his faith. Perhaps he later heard his boss, the centurion, confess, "Truly this was the Son of God." It was not the centurion alone who said that, for we read, "*They* feared greatly, saying, Truly this was the Son of God" (Matthew 27:54; emphasis added). We are left encouraged to believe that in Jesus' last hours He won not only the repentant thief but also the Roman centurion and at least one of his soldiers. Perhaps it was this man who took pity on the world's Savior in His hour of desperate need.

When Jesus was hanging on the cross, most of those who saw Him despised Him. Would you have been willing to attract the ridicule of the mob to relieve His thirst? Are you willing to step forward today and demonstrate your loyalty to Jesus when it seems everybody is against you? What happens at the cross is the moment of truth for everybody in the world. We all encounter Jesus there. It is a timeless event.

Jesus speaks to you and me just now, saying, "Whosoever . . . shall confess me before men, him will I confess also before my Father which is in heaven." Unfortunately, He must add also, "Whosoever shall deny me before men, him will I also deny before my Father which is in heaven" (Matthew 10:32, 33).

People who live in some parts of the world are well acquainted with thirst. They would consider the literal water that we so easily take for granted to be a great blessing. But in the world's deserts and in its rainforests and in every place between these two extremes—including the United States—there are people who are thirsty for the water that sustains eternal life.

As the time of Jesus' crucifixion approached, Jesus went to Jerusalem to celebrate the Feast of Tabernacles. On the last day of the gathering, He stood up and cried out for everyone to hear, "If any man thirst, let him come unto me, and drink." And then He made a promise that will lift your heart forever: "He that believeth on me, as the scripture hath said, out of his belly shall flow rivers of living water. (...This spake he of the Spirit, which they that believe on him should receive)" (John 7:37–39).

What a joy it was for Jesus to be the source of "living water" that could quench the thirst of the entire world. Now He invites you and me to experience with Him the joy of giving that water to the thirsty—of becoming little "wells of living water" out of which life-giving water flows to refresh others! If your heart is melted and you believe, you will always have something refreshing to pass on to others—some of that precious "water of life."

The last page of the Bible describes the joy you will have at last: "Let him that heareth say, Come. And let him that is athirst come. And whosoever will, let him take the water of life freely" (Revelation 22:17).

That is happiness!

Chapter 6

Saved

"It is finished!"—John 19:30

Many people believe that Jesus' death on a cross provided salvation only for the good people, the churchgoing people. It surprises them to learn that Jesus did far more: He actually saved everyone in the world!

What Jesus accomplished on the cross has been overlooked for many centuries. Realizing what it means lifts people's hearts as nothing else can. The time has come for the whole world to learn what has been misunderstood for so long—why Jesus said, "It is finished!" (John 19:30). That cry is the sixth of the seven words of hope that we are exploring together.

The question is, What was finished? Did Jesus mean that now His suffering was over and He could rest? That He had paid the debt we owe?

Yes, He meant that—and far, far more.

When Jesus was here on earth, He told people that the Father sent Him here with a specific assignment: He was to "save the world" (see John 3:17; 12:47). And John tells us that the night before Jesus died, He told the Father, "I have glorified thee on the earth: *I have finished the work which thou gavest me to do*" (John 17:4; emphasis added).

What Jesus said is good news. Because Jesus' task "is finished," we can rest secure in the knowledge that we are saved.

The Bible says that someday soon God will light the whole dark world with glory. When we study the words of Christ as He hung on the cross, we are helping to turn that plan into reality.

The Samaritans understood that truth quicker than the Jews did—in fact, quicker than the twelve disciples did. After only one meeting with Jesus, they said of Him, "This is indeed . . . the Saviour of the world" (John 4:42).

Paul understood this truth. We know that because when he wrote to Timothy, his protégé, he said that Jesus is "the Saviour of all men, specially of those that believe" (1 Timothy 4:10).

In this verse Paul speaks of Jesus being the Savior

of two groups of people. As we might expect, he says Jesus is the Savior of "those that believe." But he makes it clear that they are not the only ones whom Jesus will save. They're just a part of the "all men" that Jesus came to save. He will "specially" (*especially* in other versions) save "those that believe." But if this group who believes is part of a larger group whom Jesus will save, then there must be a sense in which He is also the Savior of people who don't believe in Him!

What Paul meant is very simple and clear. Jesus gives life to all people who live on earth during the present age, and He gives eternal life in the new earth to those who believe in Him.

The point is that even our physical lives were purchased for us by the sacrifice of the Son of God. One wise writer says that every meal we eat is in reality a sacrament, and that the cross of Christ is stamped on every loaf of bread. Most people don't realize this, for they have never been told this truth. Consequently, they "eateth . . . unworthily, . . . not discerning the Lord's body" (1 Corinthians 11:29). Jesus said, "I am that bread of life" (John 6:48). "The bread of God is he which cometh down from heaven, and giveth life unto the world" (verse 33). All life on this planet is a gift of Christ's sacrifice.

Paul tells us that "the wages of sin is death" (Romans 6:23). In fact, death would be both universal and eternal if Christ had not saved us from it. Take a deep breath and then stop and think: whether or not you deserve it (and, in fact, you don't), the simple blessing of air to breathe is a gift that Christ, "the Saviour of the world," has given you. Life would have ceased and the world itself would have perished if the Son of God had not given Himself for us. The cross of Christ made all of this possible.

A bigger picture

And there is a still larger sense in which Christ accomplished a mighty feat on His cross. It was there that He conquered Satan, the enemy of God. Satan was at one time the most beautiful of all the holy angels, but he came up with a new invention: sin. When he refused to repent, he lost his character and his position as Lucifer, the Light-bearer. So he determined that in the cosmic war of the ages that ensued, he would defeat God and take His throne for himself. This battle between Christ and Satan is known as the great controversy. It is fought in human hearts worldwide. The cross is the weapon that will defeat Satan, both in the great cosmic war and in the battle with sin in our hearts.

Revelation 12 tells us that the controversy began in heaven. It says, "There was war in heaven: Michael and his angels fought against the dragon; and the dragon fought and his angels, and prevailed not; neither was their place found anymore in heaven. And the great dragon was cast out, the old serpent, called the Devil, and Satan, which deceiveth the whole world: he was cast out into the earth, and his angels were cast out with him" (verses 7–9). (*Michael,* which means "who is like God," is one of the many names of Christ.)

Our primeval parents, Adam and Eve, believed Satan's lie and welcomed him into our world, allowing him to deceive them—and us. Now Satan's big argument is that he has invented something so powerful that even God cannot conquer it. The "something" that Satan claims is invincible is the sin that is lodged in our fallen, sinful flesh.

At times it has seemed that Satan would win the great controversy because sin has taken root so deeply in our nature that the world is full of it. All of us have been slaves of sin. "All have sinned," and "there is none righteous, no, not one" (Romans 3:23, 10). Even pastors, bishops, priests, and cardinals have succumbed to sin and have brought disgrace on Jesus. If, by our life, we proclaim that sin is stronger than the grace of Christ, we place ourselves on Satan's side in this great controversy, and our choice influences others.

One critical battle in this cosmic struggle was fought in Christ's heart during His life on earth. He was born of the virgin Mary and came in the nature of our humanity. The question was whether or not He—saddled with our infirm nature—could live a life of victory over all the temptations to sin that Satan could throw at Him.

Scripture says that Jesus was "in all points tempted like as we are." And what was the outcome? The inspired Book says He was "without sin" (Hebrews 4:15). For Him, the temptation to give in to Satan and go ahead and sin was so terribly strong that He sweated drops of blood. (I doubt that anyone else has ever done that!) It took every joule of His soul energy to say No! to Satan's alluring temptations, but Jesus emerged victorious. He "condemned sin in the flesh" (Romans 8:3). Thus He gained that glorious victory; and all who appreciate what He accomplished will pray David's prayer: "Create in me a clean heart, O God" (Psalm 51:10).

The Son of God fought this tremendous battle of the ages in His heart as He hung on a cross in the dark. He endured what no other human being in all time has had to endure—that of being, to all evidences, totally forsaken by God. He endured the total darkening of His spirit without even the tiniest ray of hope. Having been "made" to be sin though He "knew no sin" (2 Corinthians 5:21), He endured the wrath that God directs against sin. He bore all that any lost person must endure in the second death—the fate of those found to be guilty in the final judgment.

Paul says there is "the sting of death [which] is sin" (1 Corinthians 15:56). Christ bared His soul and drew that sting to Himself so that we can escape it. It can no longer hurt those who believe because it spent itself on Christ. Now, glory of glories, the throne of God is secure for all eternity to come. And by faith you and I can share the victory!

Now Christ has the right to trumpet His cry throughout the universe of God, to all the unfallen worlds, to all the holy angels, to every nook and cranny of our world, and yes, to every demon in hell: *it is finished! Satan and sin are forever vanquished.*

Does your heart rejoice in this glorious victory? Do you say "Amen"?

The victory is won "in Christ." But the battle in your heart and mine is yet to be ended in triumph over Satan and sin. On whose side do you choose to stand—that of the enemy or that of Christ?

You and I can bring glory to Christ by demonstrating that His "gospel . . . is the power of God unto salvation" (Romans 1:16) here and now. That's something worth living for!

A cry for help

"Pastor Frank, help me. I'm a terrorist!"

The cry for help seemed to rise from the very depths of the earth. In reality, it was coming from just under my feet. The young Colombian who uttered it was one among hundreds who had left their seats and come forward in response to the altar call I had given on the first night of the evangelistic meetings in Bucaramanga, Colombia.

The young man, who looked to be in his midtwenties, had managed, not without some difficulty, to place himself as close to me as he could.

I heard the cry a second time. It was breathless and desperate, like the one a drowning man might make just before sinking for the last time. As I leaned over the edge of the raised platform that had been constructed in the form of a cross, I caught a clear glimpse of the young man who had cried out.

The fact that he had phrased the cry in the present tense didn't escape my notice. "I *am* a terrorist!" he had said, not "I *used to be* a terrorist" or "*I was once* a terrorist." The threat of terrorism was the reason that a platoon of soldiers had been assigned to us, courtesy of the Colombian government. Trust me, I now wanted to know their exact whereabouts! A quick glance at the crowd, seven thousand strong, yielded neither soldiers nor the comfort I sought.

I then decided to give this "terrorist," who had called out to me, my full attention. When I turned my gaze more fully on him, the face I saw was the oldest I'd ever seen on a man so young. But nothing about the person I saw gave me cause to pause. His face told me all I needed to know: he wanted out—out of a life of violence, killings, and senseless destruction. Had he been kidnapped as a child, removed from his home, and forced to adopt the terrorist ways of his abductors? Probably. In Latin America this is an all-too-common story.

The young man called out to me again: "What can I do? Please, Pastor Frank, tell me what to do!"

Just then, the soldiers made their appearance. Two of them came right behind me and tugged gently on my vest, indicating that it was time to make the agreed-upon quick exit. And soon the gentle tug gave way to a strong pull that directed me toward the stairs at the back of the platform. All I could do for the young terrorist was to shout back, "Jesus! Jesus! Turn your life over to Jesus! He has something better for you!"

I remember praying for my young hearer long into that night. Would I see him again? Would he follow my counsel and open his heart to the Lord Jesus Christ?

On the last night of the series of meetings, the young man responded to the altar call again, standing in the very same place as he had before. That evening he said to me, with the biggest, sunniest smile I have ever seen, "Pastor Frank, pray for me. I've decided to follow Jesus and be baptized!"

Dear reader friend, Jesus came to seek and to save that which was lost. Apparently, that holds true for repentant terrorists—praise His name! He is truly the Savior of the world.

And yes, that means He is also *your* Savior and *mine*.

Chapter 7

Triumphant!

"Father, into thy hands I commend my spirit."
—Luke 23:46

The sins of the whole world through all time were laid upon Jesus. Though He was totally sinless, He had felt as responsible for them as if they were actually His. He had felt the way the people who are lost will feel when they stand before the great white throne: totally and finally condemned. Jesus had tasted death for each of us (see Hebrews 2:9)—the real thing, what the Bible calls "the second death" (see Revelation 20:14; 21:8), and that had filled Him with despair, crushing His soul.*

But Jesus progressed from that cry of forsakenness

---
* Why not stop whatever we are doing each Friday at noon and give thanks to God for what Jesus did for us? Let's call it the Friday Noon for Jesus Movement, the JC-G6-12. (The "JC" stands for Jesus Christ; the "G" for gratitude; the "6" for Friday, the sixth day of the week and the day on which Jesus was crucified; and the 12 for noon.)

to a prayer in which He expresses His total trust in His Father. God hasn't performed a miracle to renew His faith. There's been no voice from heaven. No one has given Him a word of encouragement—not even His disciples. But by faith Jesus has gained the victory. He has remembered what He learned in His study of Scripture, and His heart is at rest.

So, as the end approaches, Jesus prays, "Father, into thy hands I commend my spirit" (Luke 23:46). These are the last words He spoke before He died. They reveal that His work is done; He's ready to die. Thus He dies *triumphant!*

We must note something very important here: Jesus' last words were not His own—they were a direct quotation from Psalm 31. In that psalm David had prayed, "Into thine hand I commit my spirit: thou hast redeemed me, O Lord God of truth" (verse 5), and it was those words that were in Jesus' heart when He died.

When Jesus became Immanuel, God with us, He emptied Himself, laying aside all the prerogatives of divinity. As a baby born in Bethlehem, He had no memory of His preexistence. When He sat on Mary's lap, He didn't regale her with stories of heaven and of His adventures leading the angelic hosts. He was a true human baby. He had to learn to walk, to talk—everything that we have to learn as we grow up. All that He knew of His Father He learned from the Bible.

Jesus was the divine Son of God, but you would never have known it by looking at Him. What was different about Him was that He had so completely absorbed the Bible, which was the basis of His education, that He became "the Word made flesh." That's why what He learned from the Bible when He was a youth filled His mind in the last hour of His life. All that He had read was stored in His memory, and in the hour of His greatest need, it rose up to comfort and encourage Him. He had lived by the Word, and now He could die by the Word in perfect peace and happiness.

As was true of Jesus, when we feast upon the "bread of life"—the Word of God—the treasures of truth we consume will also become permanently etched in our memories, for Jesus has promised that His Holy Spirit will "teach you all things, and bring all things to your remembrance" (John 14:26). In other words, when Satan tries to assail our minds and hearts with temptations to doubt that Christ is your Friend and Redeemer, the Holy Spirit will flash into our minds the scriptures we have read. Fortified by the Word of God, we will be able to command Satan to get behind us just as Jesus did (see Matthew 16:23).

It is through Bible study that we identify with Jesus—that we enter into Him by faith and He enters into us. We live in Him. That's what Paul had in mind when he said, "For me to live is Christ" (Philippians 1:21). That's why David sang, "Because thou hast made the LORD, which is my refuge, even the Most High, thy habitation; there shall no evil befall thee, neither shall any plague come nigh thy dwelling.... Thou shalt tread upon the lion and adder.... Because he hath set his love upon me, therefore will I deliver him: I will set him on high, because he hath known my name. He shall call upon me, and I will answer him" (Psalm 91:9, 10, 13–15).

The Father's care for Jesus is a pledge that He will care no less for us. We need not fear death if we are ever called to face it. (We know that some believers won't die before Jesus returns, for Paul wrote that first the dead in Christ will rise, and "then we which are alive and remain shall be caught up together with them ... to meet the Lord in the air" [1 Thessalonians 4:17].) The Word of God that we have cherished in our hearts will be there in the hour when we need it, for we will have set our love upon Him (see Psalm 91:14). The Holy Spirit has appealed to us to turn away from the vanity and foolishness that pervades the world, and we will not have resisted Him; we will have welcomed Him.

But it is not merely in our last hour that the Bible brings us happiness. Through its pages, the Holy Spirit will commune with us day by day. When we are tempted by *dis*couragement, He will whisper *en*couragement to us. Jesus promised, "He shall teach you all things, and bring all things to your remembrance, whatsoever I have said unto you" (John 14:26).

Why the quote?

Do you wonder why Jesus quoted Psalm 31 in His last breath? When you read it, you will discover why: that psalm describes His experience. He saw Himself in it: "I was a reproach among all mine enemies, but especially among my neighbours, and [I was] a fear of mine acquaintance. [I scared him away.] ... I have heard the slander of many: fear was on every side: while they took counsel together against me, they devised to take away my life. But I trusted in thee, O LORD. ... My times are in thy hand. ... Let me not be ashamed, O LORD. ... I said in my haste, I am cut off from before thine eyes: nevertheless thou heardest the voice of my supplications when I cried unto thee" (verses 11, 13–15, 17, 22).

Can you begin to see how real Jesus is? How close to us He has become? That He knows our experiences, our temptations? That His heart is touched because of our weaknesses? On the cross He became the weakest and most despised person on earth. He gave Himself for us, and in His last breath He witnessed about His faith in His Father. He trusts His soul to Him. He is like David slaying Goliath; like Joseph triumphing over his brethren. He is the Lamb *triumphant* over the lion. *However, Christ doesn't conquer His kingdom by force of arms or by political intrigue, but solely by love.*

Now, in His last breath, Jesus resigns all into His Father's hands. In effect He was praying, "Resurrect Me or not, I commit My spirit, My life, My all, into Thy hands."

Jesus is the only man who has ever truly "poured out his soul unto death: and . . . was numbered with the transgressors," as Isaiah put it (Isaiah 53:12). As He hung on the cross, He wasn't thinking of the rewards that would be His when He rose again. What was uppermost in His mind as He drew His last breath was the great reward that those who believe in Him will receive.

Yes, Jesus *was* resurrected, for the Bible says that the grave could not hold Him (see Acts 2:24). Jesus' disciples thought He was dead and gone forever; but the grave couldn't hold Him. This is the basis of His pledge to us of everlasting life.

Join me in a prayer of thanksgiving and commitment to Him who "so loved" us that He gave His all for us:

Father in heaven, our hearts are so little, so childish, and yes, so selfish. Thank You for loving us so much anyway that You allowed Your Son to go to hell to find us and then to save us by dying the death that we would otherwise have had to die.

Please strengthen and enlarge our hearts so we can learn to appreciate what our salvation cost You. And give us more of that "abounding grace" so that we may honor You by living lives of obedience to You and of love for others. In Jesus' name we pray. Amen.

Chapter 8

A Bonus Word: Grateful

*"Her sins, which are many, are forgiven;
for she loved much:
but to whom little is forgiven,
the same loveth little."—Luke 7:47*

Dan Brown's novel *The Da Vinci Code* portrays Mary Magdalene as the wife of Jesus Christ and the mother of their daughter, whose descendants live among us today. The book quickly attained best-seller status, and the movie that was based on it was the second-highest grossing film of the year worldwide—no doubt in part because of their sensational claims about Mary's relationship to Jesus. In fact, soon after the book was released, *Time* magazine published a four-page feature about Mary Magdalene.

These agents of popular culture unwittingly fulfilled

Jesus' prediction about this special woman. He said, "Wheresoever this gospel shall be preached throughout the whole world, this also that she hath done shall be spoken of for a memorial of her" (Mark 14:9).

The authors of the piece in *Time* magazine glamorized Mary Magdalene to draw readers' interest. She has also been misportrayed in other books and movies by authors and actresses who do not take very seriously what the Bible says about her. The end result confuses many people.

For example, Mary has been popularly portrayed as a heroine of a "gender battle"—someone who can be used to shake up male church leadership. Many say she makes a case for women to have a more influential role in the church. Neo-pagans have even adopted Mary as a goddess. These people have invented stories about her that the Bible doesn't support.

Even Martin Luther went so far—at least once—as to suggest that Jesus and Mary Magdalene were married, says *Time*. This speculation has no biblical support. The Bible does say that eventually Jesus will marry. However, it isn't some individual woman but the church who will become His bride. No woman has been, is, or ever will be qualified to be the bride of the Son of God!

The biblical story of Mary Magdalene is fascinating.

It tells us why Jesus chose her as someone whom He could point to as a model Christian—an example to be remembered until the close of time because in what Jesus made of her we see what He wants to make of us too.

It seems that Mary started out as a happy girl in a fine family that lived in Bethany, one of the better suburbs of Jerusalem. Mary's sister was the highly competent Martha, a hostess of distinction, and her brother was the honored Lazarus, who we know had many friends and admirers, because we read that a large number of notables attended his funeral (John 11:19).

Life was good for young Mary—until she experienced a tragedy: she was abused and betrayed by a clergyman, Simon the Pharisee. The Bible doesn't say whether she was raped or seduced, but so great was her sense of shame and disgrace that she apparently ran away from home, saying something to the effect that in that place "there's nothing going nowhere."

In her discouragement, she took a nosedive into deep despair and forfeited all hope for a better life. Both Luke and Mark tell us her mind became the home of "seven devils," who tormented her to no end (see Luke 8:2; Mark 16:9). Having been ruined by one man, she apparently hated all men.

However, she had the good fortune to meet a Man who was different—Jesus Christ. She had no idea that He was the Messiah until He prayed for her and cast out a devil. Then she was overjoyed: at last there was hope for her. Little flowers began to blossom in her soul—she could again become respected.

But having one devil expelled didn't solve the problem; there were six others. Each time one was removed, she would rise with the hope that now she could overcome—only to be tripped up by another devil, and down she would go again.

It is probable that the disciples soon gave up any hope for her. They wondered why Jesus continued to work with her. Finally, the seventh devil was cast out—perhaps her obsessive hatred of the man who had ruined her life. Perhaps she was healed so completely that finally she could pray for him. When she realized that she was free, her gratitude to Jesus knew no bounds. Here was a saved sinner who was truly *grateful*!

Then Mary wondered how she could convey how thankful she was. She could not say anything in public—her reputation had been shattered. But eventually she thought of something she could do. Jesus had been telling His disciples that as the Messiah, He must suffer and die. They refused to listen to what He was saying, telling Him, "Be it far from thee, Lord" (Matthew 16:22).

But Mary's ears were open. (Often, women can hear much better than men can!) Mary resolved to purchase the finest anointing oil she could find and use it to anoint Jesus' body when He died.

The biblical description of the oil Mary bought suggests it probably was meant for a governor or an emperor. A bottle of the stuff cost three hundred silver *denarii* when one *denarius* was the wage a hard-working man was paid for a full day's labor (see Matthew 20:1, 2).

Mary made her purchase, and then, clutching her very precious alabaster flask, she headed home and placed it on a shelf, ready for the sad day when Jesus would die.

Meanwhile, something else was happening.

Another healed sinner

The man who had ruined Mary's life couldn't forget his crime. He was a Pharisee, which meant that he was highly esteemed. By day, in his office, he was all smiles and backslapping, but at night his conscience tormented him.

Then, as often happens, he became sick. Unresolved

guilt can break a person's body down, beginning with the weakest part. Simon the Pharisee was afflicted with leprosy, a dreaded skin disease that people regarded as a curse from God.

Simon had to leave home. As a leper, he knew he was disgraced in the eyes of the people around him, and worse yet, he felt that God had forsaken him forever too. However, it became his good fortune to meet the Man who had cast the seven devils out of Mary Magdalene. Jesus prayed for him, healed him of his leprosy—no questions asked—and sent him home happy.

Simon, too, wanted to say "Thank You" to Jesus for healing him, but his heart was hard as stone. For one thing, he wasn't at all sure that Jesus was the Messiah. In fact, he feared that Jesus might be a false prophet. (We can deduce this from the story as Luke tells it [see Luke 7:36–50].) Simon didn't know how to get down on his knees and shed tears of gratitude and say, "Thank You, Lord, for saving my soul." So, instead, he decided he would throw a party and invite Jesus and His lower-class disciples. That would do.

Mary wasn't on the guest list for the upcoming party, but when she heard about it, she had an idea. Why should she wait until Jesus died? Why not anoint

Him while He was still alive and knew what she was doing for Him?

So, the day of the party, Mary takes the alabaster flask down from the shelf where she had been keeping it, "crashes the gate" of Simon's house, as it were, and goes in uninvited. Impulsively and in abandon, she breaks the precious bottle and anoints not only Jesus' head, but His feet as well. A teaspoonful of that ointment would have been sufficient for honoring a guest, but Mary lavishes the whole bottle on Jesus.

A flood of tears

Then something happens that apparently Mary hasn't anticipated: a flood of tears bursts from her eyes. Never before has she cried so much. But her tears aren't flowing because of shame or fear, but because of her gratitude that Jesus has saved her soul from hell itself. Mary decides to make use of the abundant flow, so she kneels down and washes Jesus' feet with her tears. And embarrassed that she hadn't thought to bring a towel, she lets her long, full hair down (a no-no in public in that culture) and dries His feet with it.

Stunned, the host, Simon the Pharisee, watches all this without saying a word. Dark thoughts are coursing through his mind and heart though—thoughts of bitter unbelief. "When the Pharisee which had bidden him saw it, he spake within himself, saying, This man, if he were a prophet, would have known who and what manner of woman this is that toucheth him: for she is a sinner" (Luke 7:39).

Ah, yes, Simon, you great Pharisee, you should know!

I fear that had I been Jesus and known Simon's thoughts and all that lay behind them, I would have given up on him and left him to be lost. I would have said, "Simon, I have another appointment. I'll skip the dessert—I have to go."

Jesus must have arisen early that morning and prayed for the Father to guide Him, because we see that He loves Simon, too, and wants to save him as well as Mary. So the Holy Spirit gives Him a story—a priceless one that *Time* magazine completely misses! Jesus says, "Simon . . . there was a certain creditor which had two debtors: the one owed five hundred pence [denarii], and the other fifty."

Jesus is trying to reach Simon's heart. He knows that Simon will realize that he is the one who owes the five hundred, for he is the one who has committed the greater sin. He ruined Mary's life.

Jesus continues, "And when they [two] had nothing to pay, he frankly forgave them both. Tell me therefore, which of them will love him most?"

Simon begins to flush with embarrassment. "I suppose that he, to whom he forgave most" (verses 40–43).

At this Jesus fires both barrels at Simon, giving him what he deserves—and needs. Jesus directs Simon's attention to the woman kneeling at his feet and says, "Simon . . . [when] I entered into thine house, thou gavest me no water for my feet [a common courtesy at that time]: but she hath washed my feet with tears, and wiped them with the hairs of her head."

It seems likely that Jesus pauses here to let this soak in. Then He continues, "Thou gavest me no kiss [as you gave your fellow Pharisees]: but this woman since the time I came in hath not ceased to kiss my feet."

Another pause and then this: "My head . . . thou didst not anoint [not even with common cooking oil]: but this woman hath anointed my feet with [very precious] ointment" (verses 44–46).

The proud Simon is learning a lesson that all of us need to learn. Jesus states this principle of life and eternity in simple terms: "Her sins, which are many, are forgiven," which is why "she loved much." Then Jesus observes pointedly, "To whom little is forgiven, the same loveth little" (verse 47).

In essence, Jesus is saying, "Simon, there's a reason that your heart is as cold as stone. It's beause you don't know what forgiveness and gratitude are! Since you are one of the most prominent Pharisees, high up in temple society, you thought you were a righteous man. But your sin in leading Mary into ruin is ten times greater than all her sins—which are forgiven. But you haven't learned to receive forgiveness for even one sin!"

The Bible doesn't tell us whether Simon ever repented and was converted, but surely the wonderful story Jesus told could not have been fruitless!

Has your heart become hard? Would you like it to be melted by a true conversion? It can be. You must admit that your sins "are many," not few.

You may be tempted to excuse yourself because you've never been possessed by seven demons. You may be thinking, *I'm a good person for the most part: I go to church, sing in the choir, and give offerings. I know I'm a sinner, but I'm not as bad as Mary was. All I need is a little help getting over the top, and I'll be ready for heaven.*

As long as you believe that is true of you, you will be subject to the principle Jesus stated. Since you think your sins are few, you will be forever doomed to "love little."

A Bonus Word: Grateful

The truth is that none of us has even 1 percent of the righteousness we must have to be saved. Christ supplies 100 percent of that righteousness. If it weren't for the grace of Christ, we'd be no more acceptable than are any other sinners. If no Savior had come from heaven to save us, we would be in the same hell that Mary Magdalene knew. She had tasted what she had been redeemed from; that is why she loved "much." And that's why Jesus could point to her as an example of what He had come from heaven to do—to save sinners.

While Jesus was hanging on His cross in agony, Satan wrung His heart with fierce temptations. "Look, Your own people are crucifying You! Your disciples have forsaken You—one of them has betrayed You, and another has denied You with cursing and swearing. Why give Your eternal life for this ungrateful lot? You have the power! Come down from the cross, leave this ungrateful people, and go back where You belong—heaven."

Jesus was forced to admit that all Satan was saying about these people, including His own disciples, was true. But notice what He could say in reply: "Here is *one* person who understands what I am doing for the world; who knows she has been saved from hell itself. She is prophetic of many others who at the close of time will rejoice in My salvation!

"Go, Satan! I will not give up. I *will* die for the sins of the world. There will be a remnant who appreciate the 'breadth, and length, and depth, and height' of the love I am pouring out as a sacrifice" (see Ephesians 3:18).

Don't you want to be among that group?